CAMBRIDGE
UNIVERSITY PRESS

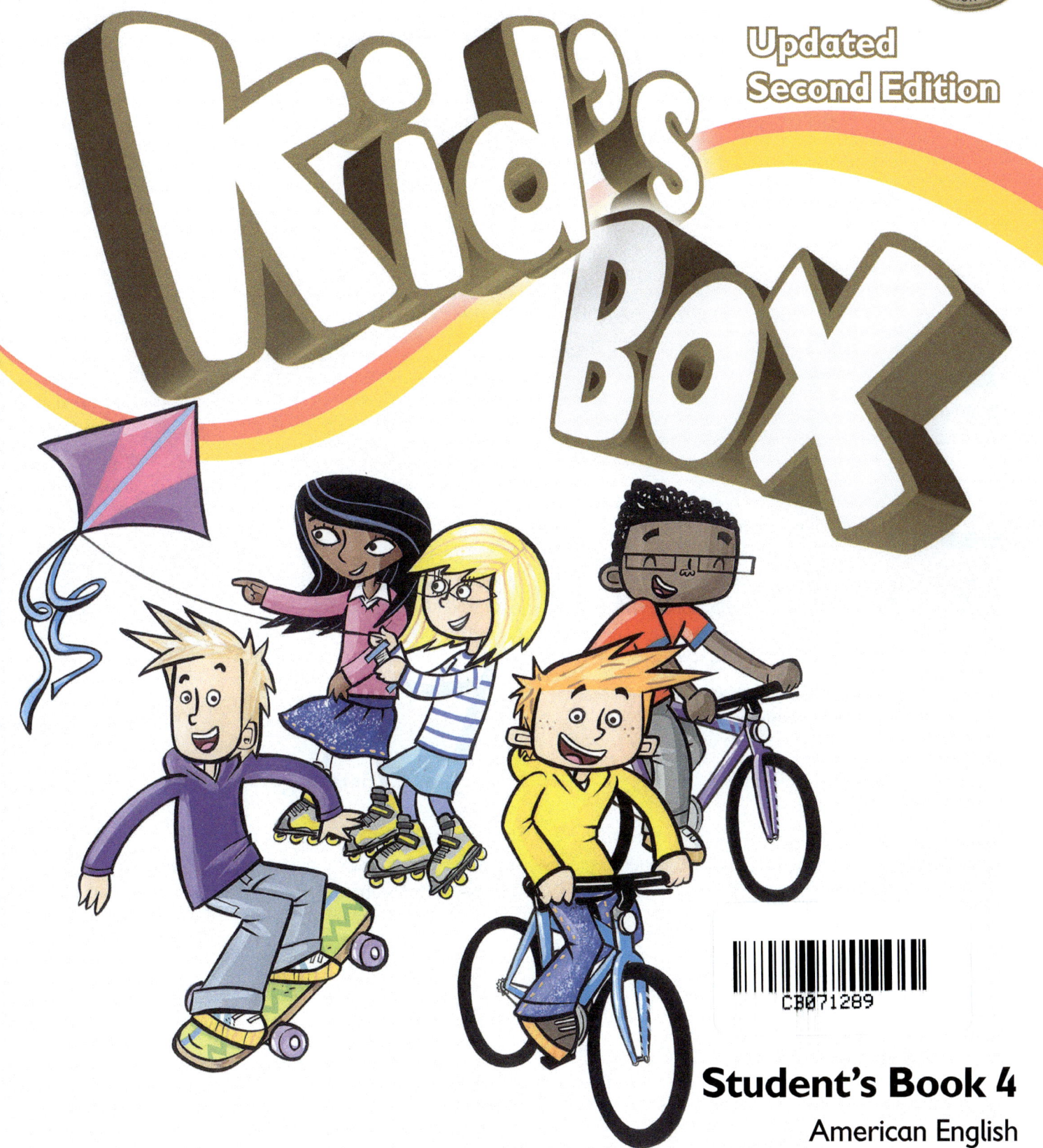

CAMBRIDGE ENGLISH
Language Assessment
Part of the University of Cambridge

CAMBRIDGE OFFICIAL PREPARATION MATERIAL

Updated Second Edition

Kid's Box

Student's Book 4

American English

Caroline Nixon & Michael Tomlinson

Language summary

	Key vocabulary	Key grammar and functions	Phonics
Hello there! page 4	Character names Personal descriptions Jobs: *farmer, dentist, detective, driver, doctor, teacher*	Comparative adjectives Simple present Frequency adverbs: *always, sometimes, never* *have to* *like/love + -ing* *want to be*	Short vowel sounds "a" (m<u>a</u>n) and "ar" (c<u>ar</u>) and long vowel sound "ai" (s<u>ay</u>)
1 Back to school page 10	Adjectives: *boring, busy, careful, difficult, easy, exciting, quick, slow, terrible*	Relative clauses with *who*	Short vowel sound "i" (qu<u>i</u>ck) and long vowel sounds "ee" and "ie" (<u>ea</u>sy and fl<u>y</u>)

Math **Measuring** page 16

	Key vocabulary	Key grammar and functions	Phonics
2 Good sports page 18	*inside, outside* Activities: *climb, dance, fish, ride, run, sail, sing, skate, skip rope, swim* Adverbs of manner: *badly, carefully, easily, happily, quickly, quietly, slowly, well*	Relative clauses with *where* *learn to do* (something) Adverbs of manner	Silent consonants (i<u>s</u>land)

Sports **Ball games** page 24   **Review 1 and 2** page 26

	Key vocabulary	Key grammar and functions	Phonics
3 Health matters page 28	Health: *dentist, have a dream, have an eye test, hospital, ill, nurse, see the doctor, take some medicine*	Simple past irregular verbs: affirmative, negative, interrogative, and short answers Clauses with *because*	Consonant sounds "b," "f," and "v" (<u>b</u>all, <u>ph</u>one, and <u>v</u>olleyball)

Music **Body percussion** page 34

	Key vocabulary	Key grammar and functions	Phonics
4 After-school club page 36	Activities: *do a musical, play chess / Ping-Pong* Ordinal numbers: *first–twentieth*	Simple past regular verbs: affirmative, negative, interrogative, and short answers Spelling of *-ed* endings	*-ed* endings "d," "id," and "t" (call<u>ed</u>, want<u>ed</u>, and kick<u>ed</u>)

English literature **Poems, plays, and novels** page 42   **Review 3 and 4** page 44

		Key vocabulary	Key grammar and functions	Phonics
5	**Exploring our world** page 46	Exploring: Antarctica, continents, exhibit, expedition, explorer, ice, make a camp, museum, field trip, ship	Simple past irregular verbs could/couldn't: ability and short answers Clauses with so Comparative of two- and three-syllable adjectives Comparative adverbs Possessive pronouns	Short vowel sound "er" (n<u>ur</u>se)
	Science • Endangered animals page 52			
6	**Technology** page 54	Technology: button, computer, DVD, email, the Internet, cell phone, mouse, MP3 player, screen, text message, turn on, video	Simple past irregular verbs	Long vowel sound "or" (sh<u>or</u>t) and long vowel sound "aw" (w<u>a</u>ter, d<u>au</u>ghter, and b<u>a</u>ll)
	Technology • Robots page 60		Review 5 and 6 page 62	
7	**At the zoo** page 64	Animals: bat, bear, bird, blue whale, crocodile, dolphin, elephant, giraffe, kangaroo, lion, lizard, monkey, panda, parrot, polar bear, rabbit, shark, snake, tiger	Superlative of two- and three-syllable adjectives Simple past irregular verbs Prepositions: behind, between, in, in front of, into, next to, on, across from, out of, under, around	Short vowel sound "oo" and long vowel sound "oo" (l<u>oo</u>k and t<u>oo</u>th)
	Science • Skeletons page 70			
8	**Let's party!** page 72	Containers: bag, bowl, bottle, box, cup, glass Food: cheese, pasta, sandwich, salad, soup, vegetables	Expressions of quantity: a cup / bag / bowl / glass / bottle / box of Superlative adverbs: the most quickly want someone to do (something)	One-, two-, and three-syllable words
	Science • Food page 78		Review 7 and 8 page 80	
	Values 1 & 2 • Value others page 82		Values 5 & 6 • Be safe page 84	
	Values 3 & 4 • Be kind page 83		Values 7 & 8 • Recycle page 85	
	Grammar reference page 86		Movers practice test page 89	

Hello there!

1 Look, think, and answer.
1. What does Sally want to be?
2. Who's a farmer?
3. What's Scott reading?
4. Who's riding Suzy's bike?

2 🔊 Listen and check.

3 Listen again. Choose the right words.
1. Sally's **twelve** / **twenty** / **ten**. *(Sally's ten.)*
2. Scott's older than **Suzy** / **Sally** / **May**.
3. Fred is Scott's **father** / **brother** / **uncle**.
4. Scott wants to be a **farmer** / **detective** / **dentist**.
5. Grandpa Star's **funny** / **young** / **sad**.
6. Aunt May's **younger** / **older** / **smaller** than Suzy.

LOOK

Sally's **older than** Scott.
Scott's **younger than** Sally.

4 Read and match. 1 – h

1. His hair is white and curly. He's funny.
2. He has short black hair, and he's wearing sunglasses. He's hungry.
3. She has straight gray hair. She's thirsty.
4. She has short brown hair, and she's young. She's little, but loud.
5. She has very long blond hair, and she's beautiful. She's quiet.
6. He has short straight red hair. He's happy.
7. She has straight blond hair, and she wears glasses. She's smart.
8. He has curly red hair, a beard, and a mustache. He smiles a lot.
9. She has straight black hair. She's tired.

5 Listen and say the name.

1 Who smiles a lot?   Uncle Fred.

6 Play the game.

Does he have red hair?   Is he younger than Sally?   Is he Uncle Fred?

Yes, he does.   No, he isn't.   Yes, he is.

7 Read and answer.

1. Where does Aunt May work?
2. What does she like doing?
3. Where does Uncle Fred live?
4. What time does he get up?

Aunt May's a doctor. She works in a big hospital in the city. She sometimes works during the day, and she sometimes has to work at night. She doesn't like working on weekends. She likes listening to music and taking pictures.

Uncle Fred's a farmer. He lives on a farm in the country. He has twenty-seven cows and forty-three sheep. He always gets up at five o'clock. Uncle Fred has to work in the morning, the afternoon, and the evening. He sometimes works at night, too. He loves working on his farm, and driving his truck!

8 Correct the sentences. (1 Aunt May's a doctor.)

1. Aunt May's a bus driver.
2. She works in a big school.
3. She never works at night.
4. She likes working on weekends.
5. Uncle Fred lives in an apartment in the city.
6. He has forty-three cows.
7. He never gets up at five o'clock.
8. He always works at night.

LOOK

She **always** wears a white coat at work.
He **sometimes** works at night.
He **never** gets up at ten o'clock.

9 **Look at the song and order the pictures. Listen and check.**

1 – b

The morning rap,
We do it every day.
The same routine,
Now listen and say.

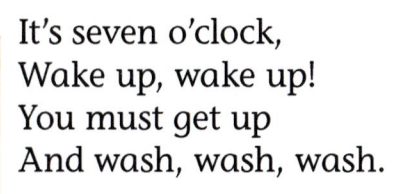

It's seven o'clock,
Wake up, wake up!
You must get up
And wash, wash, wash.

Come on, come on,
It's time to go.
Get dressed, get dressed!
Put on your clothes.

Run to the kitchen,
Sit on a chair.
Eat your breakfast,
Comb your hair.

The morning rap …

It's seven o'clock …

Brush your teeth.
No time to lose.
Get your bag,
Put on your shoes.

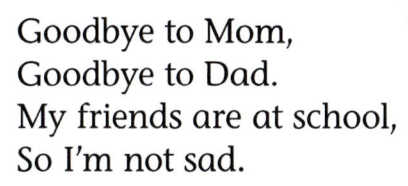

Goodbye to Mom,
Goodbye to Dad.
My friends are at school,
So I'm not sad.

The morning rap.
The morning rap.

10 **Sing the song.**

11 **Write about your day.**

I wake up at seven o'clock.
I get dressed after I get up …

12 🔊 Sally's phonics

A cat in a bag.

A snake and a snail in the rain.

A farmer in his car.

The farmer's parking his car in the parking lot.

13 Make questions. Ask and answer.

- do / have / younger cousin
- like / snails
- can / play basketball
- catch / bus / school
- can / swim
- do / have / older brother
- wake up / eight o'clock
- do / have a pet
- want to be / doctor

Do you have a younger cousin? — Yes, I do.

Do you like snails? — No, I don't.

Can you play basketball? — Yes, I can.

08
CD1
LOCK & KEY
Excuse me, Mr. Lock! This is my sister's son, Danny. He needs your help.
Hello, Danny. Well, I don't ...
No problem, Danny. What's the matter?
Detective Agency
Well, there's a picnic thief at Baker's Park.
Bah! A picnic thief ...
Let's go and see!
Right here, next to the lake. Every time I play with my friends, somebody takes our picnic.
Go and play, Danny. Put your food on the blanket. It's safe with us.
POP
Excuse me, sir. What can you tell me about the picnic thief?
Yeah, where were you at this time yesterday?
Oooh! I was at a picnic. Here in the park.
POP
Aha! So, you like picnics.
Lock, I have the picnic thief ... or, um it has me! Help!
POP
It's OK, Danny. I have your picnic.
Oh, um thank you, Mr. Key.

1 Back to school

1 Look, think, and answer.
1. Where are the children?
2. Which class are Alex and Scott in?
3. Who likes math?
4. What's Eva doing?

Scott | Alex | Sally | Robert | Eva

Art | Math | P.E.

boring   busy   careful   difficult   easy   exciting   quick   slow   terrible

2 Listen and check.

3 Listen and match.

1 Be careful with those glasses, Stacey! I am being careful! e

4 Read and correct the text.

My teacher.
This is Mr. Newton. He's my math teacher. He works at a school in a big city. He's very sbyu because he has a lot of work. There are 28 children in my class. His class isn't wols or grinbo, it's very ecgitxin. We like his class because it's not ftlcudfii. It's yase to learn a lot of new things with him.
Mr. Newton's very fclareu when he writes, but I'm not!

5 Write about one of your teachers.

6 Read and say their names.

Daisy   Fred   Mary   Johnny   Paul

1 This child likes being busy with a lot of homework. — Johnny
His hair is straight and black, and he has glasses.
2 This child loves art and is careful at painting.
He has short curly brown hair.
3 The child with straight blond hair is very brave.
She loves reading to her class!
4 This child with glasses thinks math is exciting.
Her hair is black and curly.
5 This child with short curly blond hair thinks music's difficult.

7 Make sentences for your friend. Say and answer "true" or "false."

The child with glasses thinks math is boring.   False.

8 Look, think, and answer.
1 Where is the Star family?
2 Who's Mrs. Star talking to?
3 Who's the art teacher?
4 Who's the music teacher?

Mr. Burke
Mr. Turner
Mrs. Robinson
Miss Flower
Mr. Newton

9 🎧 Listen and check.

10 Play the game.

He's the teacher who's talking to Mrs. Star.

Mr. Newton.

🔍 **LOOK**

She's the woman **who's** wearing the long green skirt.
He's the man **who's** carrying the truck.

11 Read and find.
1 They're the boys who are laughing. — d
2 She's the girl who's drinking orange juice.
3 He's the boy who's wearing a red sweater.
4 They're the girls who are wearing pink dresses.
5 She's the girl who's skipping rope.
6 He's the boy who's throwing a ball.

12 Choose a child. Ask and answer.

Is it the boy who's reading a comic book?   No, it isn't.

13 Read and say the letter. Listen and check.   1 – a

The classroom's where you learn,
The classroom's where we teach,
A lot of exciting things,
To do in our school week …

1 I teach P.E.,
It's quick, not slow,
Run, jump, and skip,
Go, go, go!

2 I teach English,
All I need,
Are a lot of words,
And books to read.

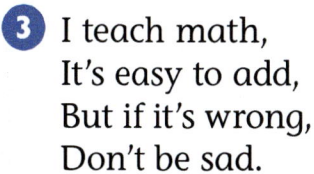

3 I teach math,
It's easy to add,
But if it's wrong,
Don't be sad.

4 I teach art,
We can paint and draw,
Careful with the paint,
Don't get it on the wall!

The classroom's where you learn,
The classroom's where we teach,
A lot of exciting things,
To do in our school week …

14 Sing the song.

15 🎵15 CD1 **Sally's phonics**

S**i**x b**u**sy **i**nsects.

A sm**i**ling crocod**i**le.

S**i**xt**ee**n t**ee**th.

It's **ea**sy to brush a sm**i**ling crocod**i**le's t**ee**th.

16 Make questions. Ask and answer.

> Do you think math is exciting?

> No, I don't.

math   art   English   difficult   exciting   easy

Find two people who …		name 1	name 2
… think math is exciting	Do you think math is exciting?		
… think art is easy	Do you think _____ ?		
… think English is difficult	Do you _____ ?		

LOCK & KEY

On Thursday we have a class about jobs. Can you come to my school to talk about your work, please?

No problem, Danny.

THURSDAY MORNING

Detectives are very important. We help people. We can find people and things.

Do you catch bad people?

Oh, yes, we can catch people who do naughty things.

Well, thank you, Mr. Lock and Mr. Key. OK children, it's lunchtime.

LUNCHTIME

Your work is very interesting. Are you very busy?

Oh, yes!

Ooops!

OK, Key. I think we have everything now. Let's go back to the office.

Look! There's a basketball. Let's play a quick game!

I need to stop the ball!

You can't get it! Score!

Well! Excuse me!

You're very naughty!

Is she a detective?

Math — Measuring

Fact: The smallest house in the U.K. is only three meters high!

1 Read and look.

length — height

We measure length and height in meters (m), centimeters (cm), and millimeters (mm). There are ten millimeters (10 mm) in a centimeter and one hundred centimeters (100 cm) in a meter.

2 Listen and say the letter. (CD1, 18)

1 Sixty-four centimeters. — f

- a 17 mm
- b 38 cm
- c 39.67 m
- d 83 m
- e 75.12 m
- f 64 cm
- g 62 mm
- h 93.56 m

3 Read and choose the answer.

1 How high is it?
  a 9.6 m
  b 96 cm
  c 96 m

2 How long is it?
  a 76.3 m
  b 42.8 m
  c 72 mm

3 How tall is it?
  a 95 cm
  b 5.9 m
  c 9.5 m

4 How tall is he?
  a 2.31 m
  b 1.8 m
  c 3.9 m

LOOK

2.45 m   two meters forty-five centimeters

16

4 Measure the things in your classroom.

pencil	11 cm
desk	
Workbook	
eraser	
me	

How long is your pencil?
How high is your desk?
How long is your Workbook?
How long is your eraser?
How tall are you?

Project Do a class survey. Draw a chart.

How tall are you?

One meter thirty centimeters.

How many children in your group …			
a are taller than 1.35 m?	How tall are you?	4
b have arms that are shorter than 60 cm?	How long are your arms?	
c have feet that are longer than 28 cm?	How long are your feet?	
d have little fingers that are shorter than 3 cm?		
e have hair that is longer than 10 cm?		

2 Good sports

1 Look, think, and answer.
1. Who do you think wants to climb?
2. How many water sports can they do?
3. Where can they do water sports?
4. Which activity can they do inside and outside?

fish
skate
swim
sail
dance
climb

Activities outside
Activities inside

2 Listen and check.

3 Listen and say the letter.   1 He's learning to skate.   h

a   b   c   d
e   f   g   h

LOOK

What can I **learn to** do?   You can **learn to** sail and fish.
It's a place **where** you can learn to play a lot of exciting sports.

4 Make five true sentences. Use the words in the boxes.

"My teacher wants to learn to climb."

I	wants to		sail.
	doesn't want to		dance.
My teacher		learn to	climb.
	want to		ice-skate.
My friends	don't want to		skip rope.

5 Say the places.

park ~~lake~~ swimming pool road ocean

1 A place where you can go ice-skating. "Lake."
2 A place where you shouldn't roller-skate.
3 A place where you can learn to swim.
4 A place where you can learn to ride a bike.
5 A place where you can learn to sail.

6 In pairs guess the place or person. You can ask only four questions.

Jim   Jack   Stacey and Paul

"Is it a person?"
"Yes, it is."
"Is it the girl who's learning to swim?"
"No, it isn't."

"Is it a place?"
"Yes, it is."
"Is it the place where you shouldn't roller-skate?"
"It's a road."
"Yes, it is."

7 Look, think, and answer.
1 Where's Mr. Star?
2 Who's climbing?
3 Where is Grandpa Star?
4 What's Suzy doing?

badly   carefully   quickly   slowly   well

8 Listen and check.

9 Read and choose the right words.
1 They're running **quietly / quickly / slowly**. *Quickly.*
2 They're shouting **loudly / quietly / carefully**.
3 He's playing **badly / loudly / well**.
4 She's riding her bike **carefully / quietly / quickly**.
5 They're reading **quietly / loudly / badly**.
6 They're running **quickly / well / slowly**.
7 He's playing **well / loudly / badly**.
8 He's riding his bike **carefully / loudly / quickly**.

10 Listen and say "yes" or "no."

1 They're playing well. — Yes.

11 Read and say the letter. Listen and check.

1 – c

Activity center,
A lot of fun.
A place to skate,
Sail, and run.
Activity center …

1 I'm skating well,
Around and around.
I'm moving quickly,
Over the ground.

Activity center,
A lot of fun.
A place to skate,
Sail, and run.
Activity center …

2 I'm climbing easily,
Up the wall.
I'm going carefully,
So I don't fall.

Activity center,
A lot of fun.
A place to skate,
Sail, and run.
Activity center …

3 We're sailing happily,
Our boat's short.
We're going slowly,
What a great sport.

Activity center,
A lot of fun.
A place to skate,
Sail, and run.
Activity center …

12 Sing the song.

13 Write another verse. Sing.

I'm **running** / **dancing** / **swimming** well,
Look at me.
Doing it **slowly** / **quickly** / **happily**,
Now you can see.

I'm dancing well,
Look at me.

14 Sally's phonics

A **sc**ien**t**is**t** is lis**t**ening to mu**s**ic.

His dau**gh**ter is eating a san**d**wich.

They shou**ld**n't clim**b** on this i**s**land!

15 Ask and find your partner.

What do you want to do?

I want to go swimming and bike riding.

What do you want to do?

I want to go climbing and sailing.

LOCK & KEY

Hello, this is the Baker Street Swim Team. Please come quickly. Somebody has our beautiful swimming trophy.

No problem. We're coming.

Look, here's the note. We have a big competition this afternoon!

"I have the swimming trophy." Aha! There are two letters here: T.S.

I have the swimming trophy. T.S.

WALK SLOWLY! DON'T RUN CLOSE TO THE POOL!

I have to shout loudly because it's difficult to hear in a swimming pool.

What? Huh?

Well, the swimming trophy isn't in the pool!

Let's go and see Mr. Sweep. He has some clean towels.

Aha! Look! Here it is! He has it! He has the swimming trophy!

Terry Sweep

Give me that cup!

Help me, Coach! Oh! The cup was nice and clean for this afternoon's competition. Now look at it!

23

Sports — Ball games

Fact: The first basketball was brown.

1 Read and match. *1 – c*

baseball   **basketball**

My favorite sport is baseball. You play baseball on (1)**a field** with (2)**a little white ball**, called a baseball. You hit the ball with (3)**a long bat**. There are two teams with nine players. One team throws and catches the ball. The other team hits the ball.

There are four bases: first base, second base, third base, and home plate. When players hit the ball, they run around the bases. When they arrive at home plate, they get a run. The winning team is the team with more runs at the end of the game.

My favorite sport is basketball. You play basketball with (4)**a big orange ball**. There are two teams with five players. Both teams try to get points by throwing the ball into (5)**a basket**, which is 3 meters above the floor.

You can throw, run, and bounce the ball, but you can't run and carry the ball at the same time. The winning team is the team with more points after 48 minutes.

2 Listen and say "baseball" or "basketball."

1 You play with a big ball.

Basketball.

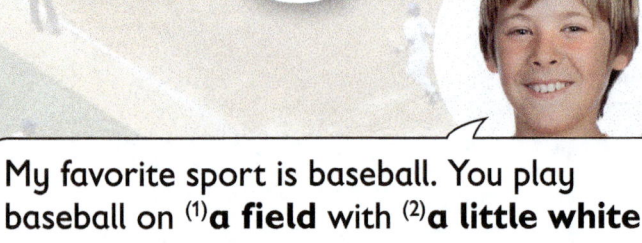

3 Do you remember? Read and answer.

Baseball
1 Where do you play baseball?
2 Do you have to play with a big orange ball?
3 How many players are there on a baseball team?
4 What do you use to hit the ball?
5 How many bases are there?
6 Which base do the players have to reach to get a run?

> You play baseball on a field.

Basketball
1 How many players are there on a basketball team?
2 Can you run and carry the ball at the same time?
3 How do you get points in basketball?
4 How many minutes do you play?

Project   Make a ball.

You need:
- 200 grams salt or sand
- 5 balloons
- scissors

1 Cut the necks off all the balloons.
2 Put the salt or sand into the first balloon.
3 Open the second balloon and put your ball inside it. Put it over the neck of the first balloon.
4 Open the third balloon and put your ball inside it.
5 Repeat with the fourth balloon.
6 Put the last balloon over the ball. Now you're ready to play.

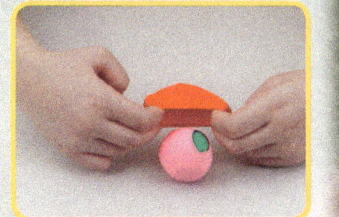

Review Units 1 and 2

1 Play the game.

Instructions

Red – Whose is it / are they?
Blue – What's this?
Gray – What's he / she doing?

2 Read the text and choose the best answer.

Example
Tony: Hi, Sue. What are you doing?
Sue: **A** I'm playing badminton.
 B I'm playing baseball.
 C I'm hitting the ball.

Questions
1 Tony: Who are you playing with?
 Sue: **A** She's my Aunt Sue.
  B My brother, Alex.
  C We're playing well.

2 Tony: Is he older than you?
 Sue: **A** No, he's my brother.
  B Yes, he's holding the ball.
  C No, he's a year younger than I am.

3 Tony: Are you good at badminton?
 Sue: **A** Yes, I have three.
  B I'm not bad, but Alex is better than I am.
  C No, thank you.

4 Sue: Do you like badminton?
 Tony: **A** Yes, it's my favorite sport.
  B Yes, please.
  C Yes, let's.

5 Sue: Would you like to play badminton with us?
 Tony: **A** I'd like that, thanks.
  B Yes, I like board games.
  C No, I prefer tennis.

6 Sue: Should I start?
 Tony: **A** Yes, I want to stop.
  B No, I want to play.
  C Yes, good idea.

Quiz!
1 Which class are Alex and Scott busy in?
2 Who's the teacher playing the guitar at the school show?
3 Where do Danny and his friends have their picnic?
4 What does Suzy want to learn?
5 How's Scott climbing?
6 Where do Lock and Key go on Thursday morning?

3 Health matters

1 Look, think, and answer.
1. What was Scott's temperature?
2. Where was Scott on Thursday?
3. Why were Scott and his mother at the hospital?
4. When was Scott well again?

Monday

Tuesday

Wednesday

Thursday

Friday

was   were   had   drank   saw   gave   took   went   ate

2 🔊 Listen and check.

3 🔊 Listen and say the day.

1 The doctor gave him some medicine.

Wednesday.

4 Read and say the letter.   1 – d

1. He took some medicine because he had a cold.
2. We ate a lot because we were hungry.
3. She went to bed early because she was sick.
4. I drank a lot because I had a temperature.
5. The doctor gave her some medicine because she had a stomachache.
6. They saw the dentist because they had a toothache.

5 Look and answer. Say "Tom," "Sue," or "the nurse."

1. Who saw the nurse?   Tom.
2. Who went to the hospital to see Tom?
3. Who had a headache?
4. Who gave Tom some medicine?
5. Who ate lunch in bed?
6. Who had an eye test?
7. Who drank orange juice?
8. Who took some medicine?

6 Look, think, and answer.

1. Who's Sally talking to this morning?
2. Where was Sally in her dream?
3. What was Sally's job?
4. What was wrong with the man?

This morning

Last night

7 🔊 Listen and check.

8 Answer the questions.

1. Did Sally have a nice dream? — No, she didn't. She had a terrible dream.
2. Did she have a long blue coat?
3. Did she see a woman who had a cough?
4. Did she give the man some flowers?
5. Did she see a woman with a backache?
6. Did she take a box off the girl's head?

LOOK

have ➡ had
do ➡ did

I **had** a terrible dream.
I **didn't have** time to stop.
How many people **did** you see?

9 **Read and say the word. Listen and check.**

> lemonade   ice cream   burgers   chocolate
> three   water   party   pizza   ~~nurse~~   fruit

Nurse

Mommy, Mommy call the 🧑‍⚕️!
I had a stomachache, but now
it's worse.

What's the matter?

I don't know,
But please be quick,
Don't be slow.

Did you have a 🎉 yesterday?

Yes! There was a lot to eat and
games to play.

Did you eat 🍔?

Yes, I did.

Did you eat 🍕?

Yes, I did.

Did you drink 🧃?

Yes, I did.

Did you have 🍨 and 🍫, too?
I think I know what's the matter
with you!
Take this medicine **3** times a day,
When you are better, go out and play!

No more chocolate for you,
my daughter.
Vegetables, 🍎🍌, and a drink of 💧!

10 **Sing the song.**

11 **Ask and answer questions about the song.**

Did she eat ice cream?

Yes, she did.

Did she drink orange juice?

No, she didn't.

12 **Sally's phonics**

A frog with a phone.

A very small volleyball.

The frog and her friends are playing volleyball at the beach.

13 Ask and answer.

Did you have a temperature last week?

No, I didn't.

Health matters

1	Did you have	a temperature last week?
2		to the hospital last year?
3		milk for breakfast?
4		a cough last year?
5		an apple yesterday?
6		to bed early last night?
7		any medicine last week?
8		the dentist last year?

~~have~~
go
eat
drink
take
see
have
go

14 Now write and ask questions about your friend's week.

Did you walk to school last week?

LOCK & KEY

So, Nick Motors, the car thief, is back in town.

Oooops! Sorry I'm late. I went to the hospital to see my Aunt Emma. She has a bad cough.

I went to the hospital gift shop. There was a man there. He had black hair and a big nose. I think it was Nick Motors, the car thief.

In the hospital? Let's go there now.

I really want to catch Nick Motors this time, Key.

No problem, Lock!

Come on! We need to go inside quickly, before he runs away.

There he is! That's him, Lock!

No, Key, he's not Nick Motors. He's a doctor.

Nick Motors isn't inside the hospital, Key. He's outside in the street ... and ...

He's taking our motorcycle!

Music | Body percussion

Fact
The quickest person in the world can clap 12 times a second.

1 🎵 CD1 39 **Listen and say the letter.**

a b c d e f

A percussion instrument is a musical instrument that makes a sound when we hit it. We can use different kinds of instruments or other things to make percussion music.

2 🎵 CD1 40 **Listen and match. Which part of the body are they using to make the sound?**

The human body is also a great percussion instrument. There are different kinds of dance and music that use parts of the body.

a b c d e f

34

The language of music tells musicians what notes to play and how to play them. They can be long or short, loud or quiet, quick or slow. Rhythm tells us how long the notes are. They can be whole notes (1), half notes ($1/2$), quarter notes ($1/4$), or eighth notes ($1/8$). Rhythm is very important in percussion music.

3 🎧 **Listen to these notes. Answer the questions.**

1 Which is longer, 1 or 4?
2 Which is longer, 2 or 3?
3 Which is shorter, 1 or 2?
4 Which is shorter, 3 or 4?

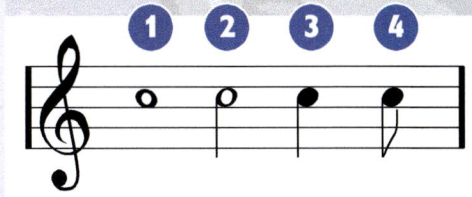

4 🎧 **Listen and make rhythms.**

Project

Make a drum.

You need:
- a plastic cup
- a balloon
- a rubber band

1 Take a piece of the balloon and put it over the top of the cup.
2 Use the rubber band to keep it in place. Now you have a drum.

Try to make different sounds. Hit it with your hand or with a pencil. Hit it in the middle or on the edge. Try different rhythms. Play your drum to music.

4 After-school club

1 Look, think, and answer.

1. Where did the children go yesterday afternoon?
2. Which teacher was there?
3. Who did Sally play chess with?
4. Who wasn't good at dancing?

2 🔊 Listen and check.

3 🔊 Listen and say "yes" or "no."

1 The children helped Mr. Star.

No.

LOOK

help	→	help**ed**
dance	→	danc**ed**
stop	→	stop**ped**
carry	→	carr**ied**

4 Read and match.

1 When Pat worked at a school, she was the cook. She made all the food in the morning. The children liked eating her pancakes! After lunch, Pat helped the children as they hopped, skipped and jumped on the playground.

2 Tod lived in the country. He loved sports, and he climbed and sailed every weekend. When it rained, he called his friend, Fred, and they played badminton inside.

3 Yesterday David invited his friend Sid to go ice-skating. It was very cold, so they needed hats and scarves. It started to snow, but Sid ice-skated on the lake. David pointed and shouted because Sid wasn't careful.

5 Listen and say a, b, or c.

1 It started to snow.   b

6 Ask and answer.

1 Where did Pat work?
2 When did Pat cook?
3 Who loved Pat's pancakes?
4 Where did Tod live?
5 What did Tod love?
6 What did Tod and Fred play?
7 Who did David invite?
8 Why did David point and shout?

She worked at a school.

7 Look, think, and answer.

1. Which friend are the children visiting?
2. Where is Alex's apartment?
3. Who loves climbing?
4. Why must they walk up the stairs?

8 Listen and check.

9 Answer the questions.

1. What's the third letter of the alphabet? — c
2. What's the ninth letter?
3. What's the twelfth letter?
4. What's the sixteenth letter?
5. What's the twentieth letter?

10 Write more questions to ask your friend.

LOOK

first	1st
second	2nd
third	3rd
fourth	4th
fifth	5th

11 Listen and complete the song.

Dancing is good, dancing is fine,
Dancing is great!
Come on, children! Dance in line!

First, second, third, and fourth
Dance, dance across the floor.
_____, sixth, seventh, _____
Jump, kick, don't come in late.
_____, tenth, eleventh, _____
Dancing is _____ for your health.

Dancing's good, dancing's fine,
Come on, children! Dance in line!

Number five's _____,
And number ten's last.
He can't hop and skip,
He can't get past.

Dancing is good, dancing is fine,
Dancing is great!
Come on, children! Dance in line!

12 Sing the song.

13 Ask and answer.

Which team was first last week?

Kids United.

SOCCER LEAGUE CHART

1 Kids United	8 Sports Kids	15 Walking Legs
2 Star Athletic	9 Quick Kickers	16 The Hungry Sharks
3 Heart Club	10 Dream Team	17 The Goal Monsters
4 All Sports	11 Great Movers	18 Naughty Monkeys
5 Healthy City	12 Cambridge Flyers	19 The Terrible Tigers
6 Box Runners	13 The Non Starters	20 Feet First
7 Sporting	14 Dirty Players	

14 **Sally's phonics**

Yesterday, Sam and Pam play**ed** soccer.

Sam got the ball and kick**ed** it to Pam.

Oh, no! They need**ed** that goal!

15 Make questions. Ask and answer.

Did you dance to music last week?

Did you watch TV in your room last week?

Yes, I did.

No, I didn't.

walk play listen	~~to music~~ to the radio to school
help ~~watch~~ take	your mom a picture your homework
~~dance~~ do practice	Ping-Pong ~~TV in your room~~ roller-skating

Find two people who … last week		name 1	name 2
… dance to music	Did you dance to music last week?		
… watch TV in your room	Did you watch TV in your room last week?		

10
CD2
LOCK & KEY
Hello, Danny. What are you doing here?
I have two tickets for my school show on Wednesday. Would you like to come?
Detective Agency
Yes, please, Danny. Which show are you doing?
We're doing Peter Pan. Students and parents are in it.
We're over there in the fifth row. These are our chairs. Can you go and get us some drinks, Key?
No problem, Lock! Two lemonades.
This is great!
Look at him, Key! It's Nick Motors!
I crossed the ocean and sailed to Neverland to catch you, Peter Pan!
Come down here! You, you, you ... pirate!
I know who you are! Oops!
Ow, my beard. That hurts!
Dad, this is Mr. Lock. Um, Mr. Lock, this is my dad.

English literature — Poems, plays, and novels

1 Read and match.

Fact
The biggest book in the world is an atlas in the British Museum. It's 1.8 m high!

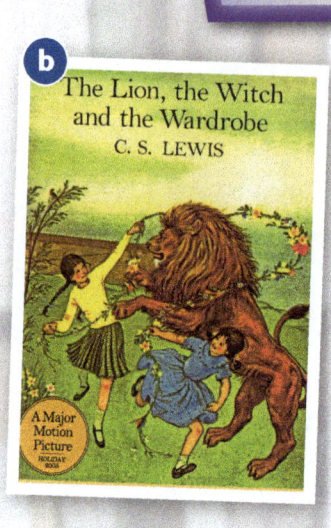

a

b

c

There are a lot of different kinds of literature. What do you like reading?

1 Poems
The Owl and the Pussycat is a children's poem by Edward Lear.

> The Owl and the Pussycat went to sea
> In a beautiful pea-green boat,
> They took some honey, and plenty of money,
> Wrapped up in a five pound note.

2 Plays
We go to a theater to see plays. *Peter Pan* by J. M. Barrie is a famous children's play about the adventures of Peter Pan, Wendy, and her brothers, John and Michael. They learn to fly and go to the island of Neverland, where they fight Captain Hook and his pirates.

3 Novels
C. S. Lewis is the author of *The Chronicles of Narnia*. There are seven books in *The Chronicles of Narnia*. The first is *The Lion, the Witch and the Wardrobe*. It is about the adventures of the Pevensie children in the country of Narnia.

2 Answer the questions.
1. What color was the Owl and the Pussycat's boat?
2. Where does Peter Pan fight Captain Hook?
3. How many books are there in *The Chronicles of Narnia*?

3 Read and order the text. 1 – d

The Lion, the Witch and the Wardrobe

a One of the rooms had nothing inside it except a big old closet for clothes – a wardrobe. Lucy went inside, and she saw a lot of coats. She walked to the back of the wardrobe.

b Lucy went back to Narnia with the other children. They helped the king, a lion, to make Narnia a happy place. Later, Peter, Susan, Edmund, and Lucy were kings and queens of Narnia.

c Then there was snow on the ground, and trees touched her face. Lucy was cold. She was in a forest at night. The wardrobe was behind her. Lucy was in Narnia, where animals can talk. One of them told Lucy that a bad white witch lived in Narnia and it was always winter. All the animals were sad.

d Four children went to stay in a big house in the country. Their names were Peter, Susan, Edmund, and Lucy. One day it was very rainy outside, so they played inside. It was boring, but the house had a lot of rooms to look in.

Project Make a "My favorite book" poster.

My favorite book
My favorite book is called ....
The author's name is ....
The story is about ....
The characters are named ....
I like it because ....

Review Units 3 and 4

1 Play the game.

Instructions
Before you play, decide which actions are good and which are bad.
Good actions: Go forward 2 spaces.
Bad actions: Go back 2 spaces.

FINISH

- You helped your mom.
- You didn't do your homework.
- You went to soccer practice.
- You worked quickly and well.
- You talked to your friend in class.
- You were naughty in class.
- You cleaned your room.
- You were late for school because you stopped to buy a comic book.
- You answered your grandpa's email.
- You carried the groceries for your grandma.

START

2 How did Mary go to these places?
Listen and write a letter in each box. There is one example.

train	H	car
walking		bus
bike		boat

A B C D
E F G H

5 Exploring our world

1 Look at Scott's homework. Think and answer.
1. Who did Scott show his homework to?
2. Who did Scott write about?
3. Who was Shackleton?
4. How did Shackleton go to Antarctica?

A famous explorer, Sir Ernest Shackleton, wanted to cross Antarctica. In 1914 he started the expedition, but ice closed around the ship. They took smaller boats and made a camp on the snow. They lost their ship when it went down under the ice and water.

They couldn't move because the weather was terrible. They caught fish and drank water that they got from snow. Later, they had to eat their dogs.

Shackleton and some of his men climbed over mountains of ice, found help, and went back for the other men. Everybody came home two years after the start of their expedition. They didn't cross Antarctica.

Ernest Shackleton

2 Read and check.

3 Find the past of these verbs in the text.

find   catch   take   go   make
get   can't   lose   have to   come

4 Read and say the letter. 1 – f

1. Last week David's class went to a museum.
2. First they walked around an exhibit about explorers.
3. They could read explorers' diaries, so it was really exciting.
4. Before lunch they made a poster about famous explorers.
5. After lunch they found the museum gift shop, and David got a toy polar bear for his sister.
6. In the afternoon they went to an exhibit about sea animals.
7. Before they came home, David took a picture of his friends.
8. At three o'clock they caught the bus home.

5 Listen and answer the questions.

1 When did David's class go to a museum?

They went to a museum last week.

6 Make sentences. They were hungry, so they ate sandwiches.

	so	
1 They were hungry,		they couldn't find the museum.
2 They didn't take water with them,		he got a toy from the gift shop.
3 The exhibit was really good,		they ate sandwiches.
4 It was his sister's birthday,		they came home late.
5 The children had to wait for the bus,		they had a great time.
6 They lost their map,		they were thirsty.

47

7 Look, think, and answer.

1. Which explorers are Scott and Alex talking about?
2. What was Cousteau's ship called?
3. Who did Alex write about?
4. What did Cousteau explore?

Cousteau

Shackleton

8 🔊 Listen and check.

9 Complete the text.

Alex thinks that Shackleton's adventures were ___more___ difficult _____ Cousteau's, but Cousteau is _____ famous for his work. Cousteau said we have to be _____ careful with the ocean. Sally thinks Scott's homework was _____ interesting _____ hers. Robert was happy because he did his homework _____ quickly than Scott and Alex.

> **LOOK**
> Cousteau is **more famous** for his work.
> Our homework was **easier than** theirs.
> Shackleton sailed **more slowly than** Cousteau.

10 Order the words.

1 interesting / My book on explorers is / yours. / than / more
2 dangerous / more / Jacques Cousteau's. / than / Shackleton's adventures were
3 more / climbing trees. / Crossing Antarctica is / difficult / than
4 than / Jacques Cousteau. / more / Christopher Columbus is / famous
5 carefully / Suzy. / more / Scott writes / than
6 walking. / Sailing is / exciting / more / than

11 What do you think? Make sentences.

boring   exciting   dangerous   beautiful   difficult   easy

I think climbing is more dangerous than swimming.

climbing   swimming   pop music   classical music

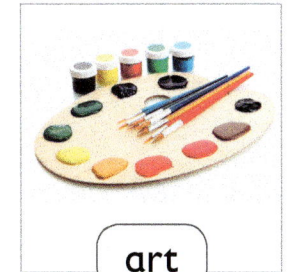

math   art   badminton   Ping-Pong

horses   fish   picture   painting

12 Now write sentences.

I think badminton is more boring than Ping-Pong.

13 Sally's phonics

The nurse got a shirt for her birthday.

On Thursday the shirt got dirty.

The nurse worked in her purple shirt.

14 Complete the rap. Listen and check.

trees   green   ~~mine~~   ours   his   strong

The world isn't **mine**,
The world isn't yours.
The world isn't _____,
The world isn't hers.
It's ours,
It's _____!

Our world is tired, we're making mistakes,
We need our oceans, we need our lakes.
Our world is weak, we can make it _____,
It needs our help. Listen to our song.

We must take care of its forests and _____,
We must take care of its rivers and seas.
We can make it better, we can make it _____.
This is our world, let's keep it clean.

15 Sing the song.

LOCK & KEY

19 CD2

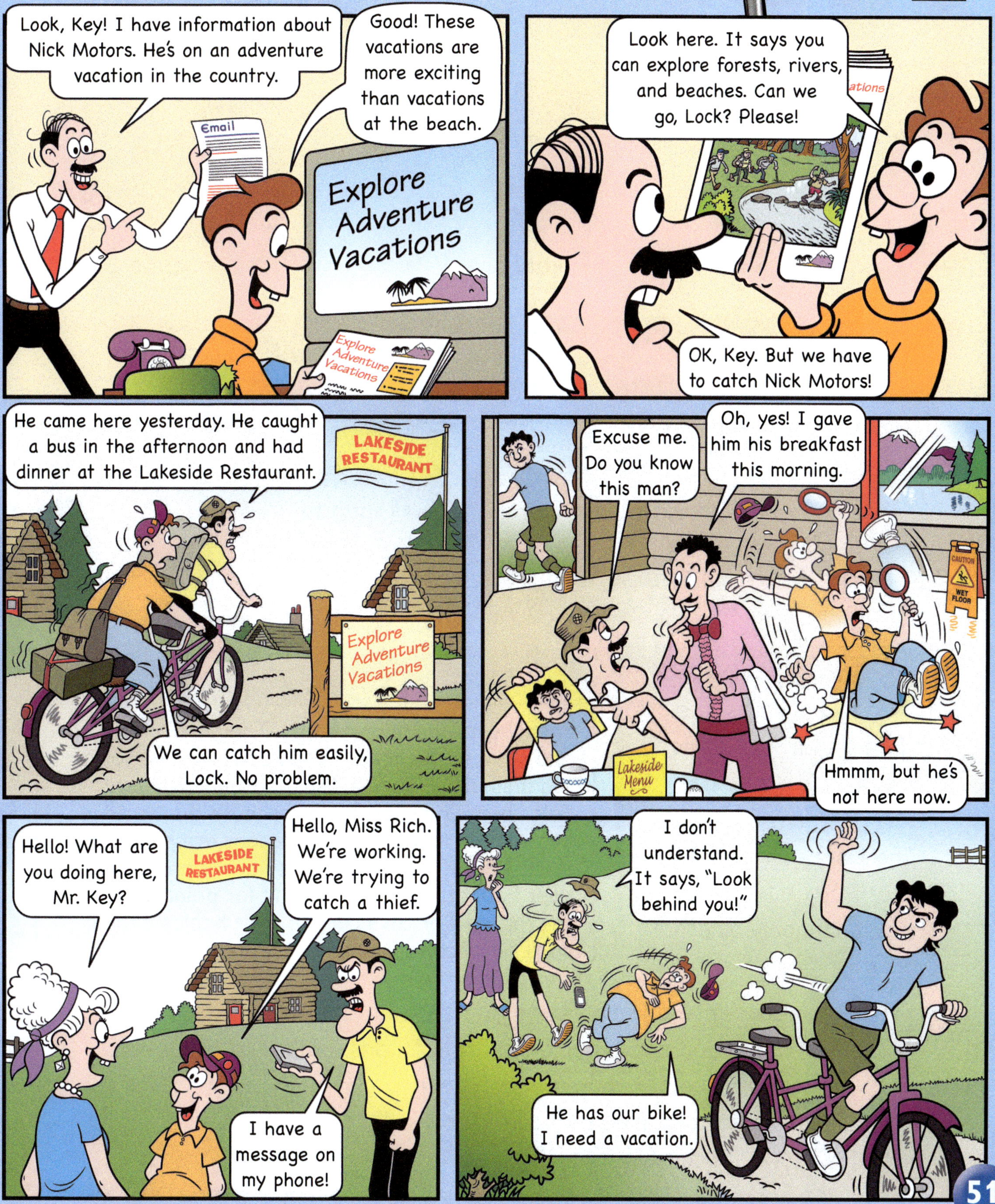

Science — Endangered animals

Fact: The name "Arctic" comes from a Greek word meaning "close to the bear."

1 Look. Which animals do you think are endangered?

- polar bear
- kangaroo 
- goat 
- Siberian tiger 
- panda 

2 Read. Correct the sentences.

Lily wants to help the world. She wants to stop the earth from getting hotter and the Arctic from getting smaller. She's in a society called the Green Heroes. They help endangered animals.

Polar bears live in the Arctic. They live on the ice and swim in the ocean. They catch and eat other sea animals, like seals, fish, and small whales. Polar bears have problems because the world is hotter than it was before. Oceans are hotter and the ice cap is smaller, so polar bears are losing their habitat. It's more difficult for polar bears to fish for food or take care of their babies if they don't have ice to live on.

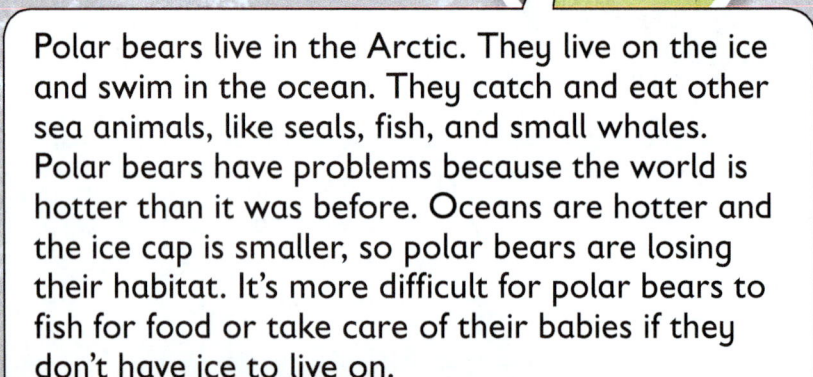

1. Polar bears live on mountains and swim in the lake.
2. They catch and eat other animals, like lions, bats, and pandas.
3. The world is colder than it was before.
4. It's easier for polar bears to fish for food.
5. It's more difficult for polar bears to take care of their parents.

3 [20 CD2] Listen. Read and say "yes" or "no."

Listen to Lily talking to a friend about the society and their work.
1. Lily's project is called "Help the World."
2. The Green Heroes are young people who want to protect cars.
3. The earth is getting colder.
4. Air in big cities is cleaner now.
5. It's a good idea to ride bikes and use public transportation.
6. People are cutting down trees in forests.
7. The world needs trees to clean the air.

Project Make a poster about endangered animals.

- Choose three endangered animals.
  You can use whale, dolphin, panda, penguin, polar bear, tiger, or elephant.
- Write an article about your animals, then make a poster. Use the words in the boxes.

in forests   in the ocean   in rivers and lakes   on the ice cap

smaller   hotter   drier   dirtier

6 Technology

1 Look, think, and answer.
1. What's Sally talking about?
2. Who wants to learn about computers?
3. Who knows about computers?
4. Who's thinking about music?

Labels: email, screen, the Internet, DVD, button, computer, mouse, MP3 player

2 🎧 Listen and check.

3 🎧 Listen and repeat. Say the letter.

"1 Screen" — "Screen – c"

a. b. c. d. e. f.

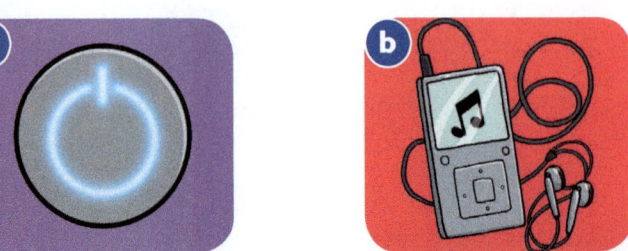

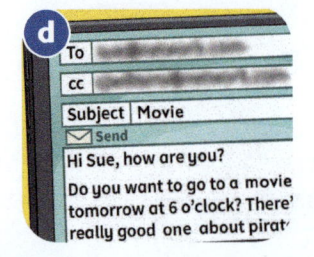

4 **Listen and match.** 1 – e

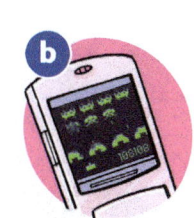

Grandpa needs a new cell phone, (No, I don't!)
With an MP3. (A what?)
It has music and (1) video clips,
And a lot more to see. (I don't need any more!)

Grandpa needs a new cell phone, (No, I don't!)
So he can (2) text his friends. (I can talk to my friends!)
He can take a lot of (3) pictures,
And play (4) games on the weekends. (I go fishing on the weekends!)

Grandpa! (I have a DVD player at home!)
Grandpa! (I have a nice camera!)
Grandpa! (And my old cell phone works perfectly well!)
Grandpa needs a new cell phone. (A new cell phone!)

Grandpa needs a new cell phone, (No, I don't!)
So he can (5) plan his day. (I have a pen and paper!)
He can listen to a lot of (6) songs,
And (7) call or even play. (I don't have time to play! I have a radio!
I have a nice camera! My old cell phone works perfectly well! Hmph!)

5 **Sing the song.**

6 **Ask and answer. Use the words in the box.**

Does your grandpa have a cell phone?
No, he doesn't.
Can you use a computer?
Yes, I can.

computer   TV   camera   the Internet
cell phone   email   e-book   video   app

7 Look, think, and answer.
1. Where did Grandma and Grandpa go yesterday?
2. What did they get?
3. What's their computer called?
4. What problem do they have?

8 Listen and check.

9 Complete the text.

said   knew   put   ~~bought~~   thought   read   brought   chose

Grandma and Grandpa went shopping yesterday. They bought a computer. They chose a KBX4 because Grandma _____ about it, and the man in the store _____ it was better than the others. The man _____ it home later. He took it out of the box, _____ it on the table, and _____ goodbye. He thought they _____ the KBX4 because they _____ about computers!

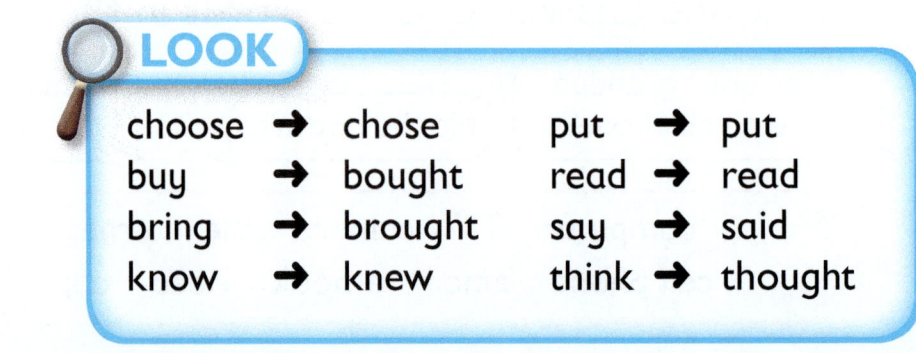

LOOK

choose	→	chose	put	→	put
buy	→	bought	read	→	read
bring	→	brought	say	→	said
know	→	knew	think	→	thought

10 🎧 **Listen and correct the actions.**

Jim has a new computer game called Kid City. The people in his game do different things every day. Look at what they did yesterday.

> At seven o'clock John got dressed.

> No. At seven o'clock John got up.

yesterday

1. John
2. Mary
3. John
4. Jack
5. Danny, Sue
6. Jack
7. Mary
8. Mary
9. Sue
10. Danny
11. Mary
12. Danny

11 **Look at the pictures. Ask and answer.**

> What time did Mary get dressed?

> She got dressed at eight o'clock.

12 **Write sentences about your day yesterday. Tell your friend.**

I got up at seven o'clock yesterday.

13 Sally's phonics

Paul caught a short fish.

His daughter bought a small ball.

The fish played with the ball in the water.

14 Make questions. Ask and find your partner.

What did you do yesterday morning?

I got up at eight o'clock …

What did you do yesterday morning?

I got up at seven o'clock …

LOCK & KEY

I need your help!

What can we do for you, Miss Rich?

A man came onto my boat and took all the money. You must catch him!

No problem, Miss Rich!

The money was for my "Save The Ocean Society." Here's the DVD of the inside of the boat.

Let's look at it.

Ooooops!

I had the money in a bag ready to put into the bank. It was on the table.

Here's the man now.

It's Nick Motors!

So Nick Motors is more than a car thief!

Well, cars are more difficult to take than money.

Hey! Motors wrote an email. We can read it!

Hello, Lock. Nice to see you again. Thanks a lot. Nick.

Um, Lock, I think you need to look outside!

Oh! Aagh!

Noooo! He has our boat, too!

Bye bye, boys. The water is great! Have a nice swim!

59

Technology — Robots

Fact: The first humanoid robot was designed by Leonardo da Vinci, in 1495.

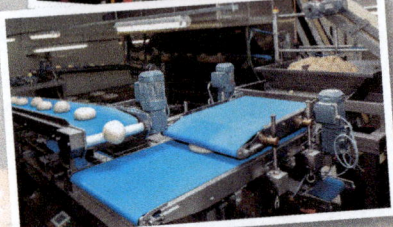

1 Read and match.

a   b   c

1 At home we have a lot of machines. There are machines that clean the floor, wash and dry our clothes, and wash the plates. In the kitchen there are machines that can make our breakfast, lunch, and dinner. Some people call these machines kitchen robots, but what is a robot?

2 A robot is a machine that makes work easier for humans. They do jobs that humans can't do because the jobs are very difficult or dangerous. Robots can explore places where humans can't go. They can go where there are dangerous gases or high temperatures: underground, underwater, and in space.

3 Robots are very important because they make, build, and fix things. It's easier for robots to work in factories because they can do the same job again and again and it isn't boring for them. Robots don't need money or vacations, and they are never sick or tired. But they can't think. Robots can do only what humans program them to do.

2 🔊 CD2 31 Listen and say "yes" or "no."

3 Read and match. Answer the questions.

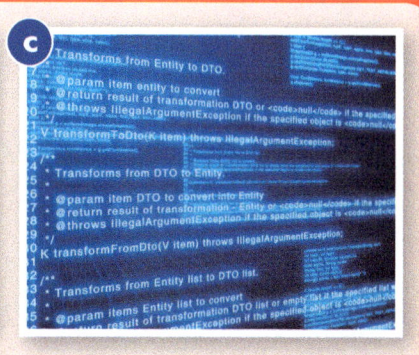

a b c

Robots aren't the same as humans. They don't have bodies like ours, but they have three important parts.

① They have a computer program. This tells the robot what to do.
② They sometimes have legs that can make the robot move along the floor.
③ They have sensors. The sensors help the robot "see" and know where things are. The sensors are sometimes cameras.

1 How many important parts do robots have?
2 What tells the robot what to do?
3 What can make the robot move?
4 What helps the robot know where things are?
5 Where can the robot move?

Project — Design a robot.

Review Units 5 and 6

1 Play the game. What did they do yesterday?

Instructions
1. Roll the die and go around the board.
2. Say what each person did yesterday.
3. If your sentence is correct, stay where you are.
4. If your sentence is wrong, go back to where you were.

2 Read the story and complete the sentences. Use 1, 2, or 3 words.

Shopping trip
Last Wednesday Alex went shopping with his mother, Pat. They went downtown by bus and had a burger in a café before they went shopping. Alex's mom wanted to buy a new bike for his younger sister, Jill. It was her birthday on Friday. The name of the toy store was Pete's Toys. They bought Jill a new red bike and took it home on the bus.

1 Alex and __his mother__ went shopping last Wednesday.
2 They ate _____ in a café.
3 Jill is Alex's _____.
4 They bought Jill _____.
5 On Friday it was _____ birthday.
6 Jill's bike was _____.
7 They went home _____.

Quiz!
1 How did Shackleton and his men lose their ship?
2 Who is more famous for his work, Cousteau or Shackleton?
3 Where did Nick Motors have dinner?
4 What do you hold in your hand when you use a computer?
5 Which computer did Grandma and Grandpa buy?
6 What did Nick Motors write?

63

7 At the zoo

1 Look, think, and answer.

1 What are Robert and Sally doing?
2 Who's asking the questions?
3 What's the quiz about?
4 Who do you think is winning?

2 🎧 Listen and check.

3 🎧 Listen and say "yes" or "no."

1 Robert thinks the most exciting animal is the giraffe.

No.

LOOK

quick	→ the **quickest**
big	→ the **biggest**
exciting	→ the **most exciting**
beautiful	→ the **most beautiful**
good	→ the **best**

4 **Read and correct.**

Fred's Blog

Animals are one of the most interesting things to watch and study. A lot of people think that elephants are the biggest animals in the world, but the biggest animals are blue whales. They're the longest, biggest, and loudest of all animals. They're louder than planes.

One of the smallest animals in the world is a lizard. It's between one and two centimeters long. The quickest animal is a bird that can fly at more than three hundred kilometers an hour.

The smartest animals are humans, that's us! Some people think that monkeys are the second smartest, but they aren't. Dolphins are smarter than monkeys.

My favorite animals are tigers. I think they're the most exciting and most beautiful animals.

1 Kangaroos are the biggest animals.
2 Bears are the loudest animals.
3 One of the smallest animals in the world is a rabbit.
4 The quickest animals are lizards.
5 Monkeys are the second smartest animals.
6 Fred thinks pandas are the most exciting animals.

5 **What do you think? Write sentences.**

beautiful   exciting   boring   smart   ugly   dangerous

I think the rabbit is the most boring animal here.

65

6 Look, think, and answer.

1. Where did the children go?
2. Who did Suzy give her picture to?
3. What animals did they feed?
4. Which animal did Scott like the best?

drew   came   drove   saw   swam   slept   went
flew   bought   sat   caught   ate   ran   fed

7 Listen and check.

8 Listen and say the letter.

1 Mr. Star drove the children to the zoo.

a

LOOK

What **did** he **buy**?
He **bought** a toy parrot.
He **didn't buy** ice cream.

9 🔊 **Listen and do the actions.**

10 🔊 **Listen and sing.**

The elephants drank, drank, drank,
The parrots flew, flew, flew,
The dolphins swam, swam, swam,
At the zoo, zoo, zoo.

The elephants drank, drank, drank,
The parrots flew, flew, flew,
The dolphins swam, swam, swam,
At the zoo, zoo, zoo.

What did you do,
What did you do,
What did you do,
When you saw, saw, saw them
At the zoo, zoo, zoo?

The monkeys ate, ate, ate,
The children drew, drew, drew,
The lions slept, slept, slept,
At the zoo, zoo, zoo.

The monkeys ate, ate, ate,
The children drew, drew, drew,
The lions slept, slept, slept,
At the zoo, zoo, zoo.

What did you do,
What did you do,
What did you do,
When you saw, saw, saw them
At the zoo, zoo, zoo?

When you saw, saw, saw them
At the zoo, zoo, zoo?

11 Write another verse for the song.

The crocodiles smiled, smiled, smiled,
The giraffes ………, ………, ………,
The tigers ………, ………, ………,
At the zoo, zoo, zoo.

crocodile giraffe
tiger panda
snake bat

smile dance
jump laugh
climb hop

LOOK

out of    into    round    along

12 Sally's phonics

Sue's a kangaroo at the zoo.

She's looking in her cookbook.

Look! The animals at the zoo love Sue's blue juice!

13 Make questions. Ask and answer.

Which animal is the loudest?

I think elephants are the loudest.

snail   shark   panda   penguin
kangaroo   elephant

ugliest   slowest   most dangerous
quickest   loudest   smallest

Which animal is the … ?	name 1	name 2	name 3	name 4	name 5	name 6
loudest						
most dangerous						

LOCK & KEY

Panel 1:
- Nick Motors. Now you're the most wanted man in town.
- Excuse me.
- ♪ RING! ♪

Panel 2:
- Lock here.
- Mr. Lock, I'm calling from the City Zoo. Please come quickly. We need your help.

Panel 3:
- Come on, Key. It's not the best time to play with Miss Rich's dog. We have a job to do!
- Ooops! Aagh! Ouch!
- No problem, Lock. Um, goodbye, Miss Rich.

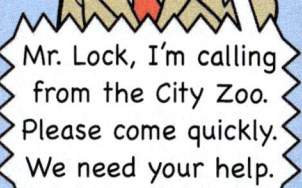

Panel 4:
- What's the problem, sir?
- A man took one of our trucks from outside the snake house.
- Was this the man?

Panel 5:
- Yes! That's him! He rode into the zoo on that motorcycle, and he drove out of it in our truck!

Panel 6:
- My motorcycle! My motorcycle!
- We can catch this thief **and** get the truck for you.

Panel 7:
- Ha, ha, ha!
- Hee, hee, hee!

Panel 8:
- Oh! The thief has the biggest problem! There was a tiger inside the truck!
- Nice cat! Oooh, Mommy!
- ROAR! SNARL!

Science — Skeletons

Fact: Instead of bones, sharks have a skeleton made from cartilage.

1 Look and read. Correct the sentences.

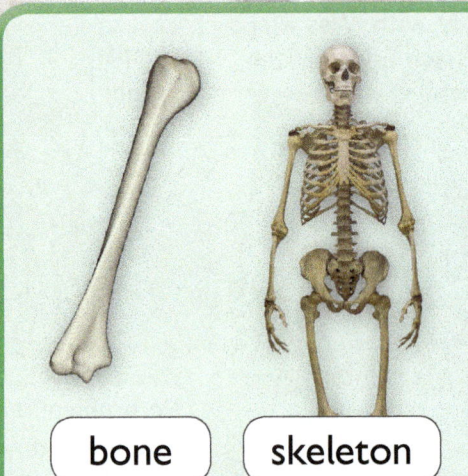

There are 206 bones in the human body. More than half of these are in the hands and feet. Bones are about 22 percent water. The smallest bone in the body is in the ear, and the longest bone is in the leg. Most bones have calcium in them. Human skeletons aren't very different from the skeletons of other animals. A human has the same number of neck bones as a giraffe!

bone   skeleton

1 There are two hundred bones in the human body.
2 All our bones are in our hands and feet.
3 The smallest bone in our body is in the arm.
4 The shortest bone is in the leg.
5 A human has the same number of foot bones as a giraffe.

2 Look at the four skeletons. Which animals are they from?

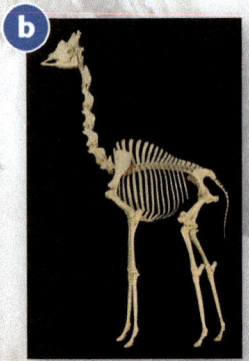

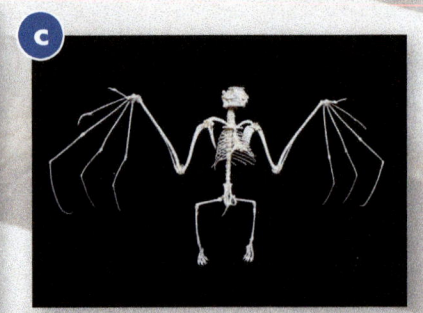

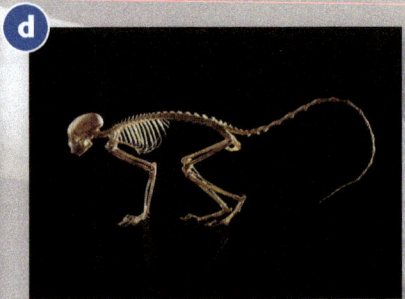

a   b   c   d

3 Read and match the animals to the skeletons.

1 This animal has very long, strong wings to help it fly quickly.
2 This animal has long arms and legs to climb trees in the jungle.
3 This animal has a very long tail to help it stand up.
4 This animal has very long neck bones to eat leaves from high trees.

4 Read and complete.

giraffes   tail   Monkeys   long   Crocodiles   skeletons

Different animals have different _____. This is because they live in different habitats, and they have to do different things to live. Some animals fly, some swim, some run, some jump, and some climb. _____ have long, strong _____ bones. These help them move quickly when they catch animals to eat. They also have big eyes on the top of their heads. These stay out of the water looking for food when the rest of its body is under water. The leaves that _____ eat are at the top of high trees, so they need very _____ neck bones to get them. _____ often have long arms, legs, and tails. These help them climb and move more quickly from tree to tree. They sometimes need to run away from other bigger, hungrier animals!

5 Listen and say "yes" or "no."

Project

Make a class comic book of "Super Animals."

- Think of two or three different animals and their skeletons.
- What can they do with their different bones and body parts?
- What's your Super Animal called?
- What body parts does it have?
- What can it do?

8 Let's party!

1 Look, think, and answer.
1. Whose birthday is it today?
2. What are the grown-ups doing?
3. What kind of sandwiches are there?
4. Who's thirsty?

bottle
box
bowl
carton
vegetables
soup
cheese
sandwich
salad
pasta
cup
glass

2 Listen and check.

3 Listen and say the letter.

1 A bowl of salad. a

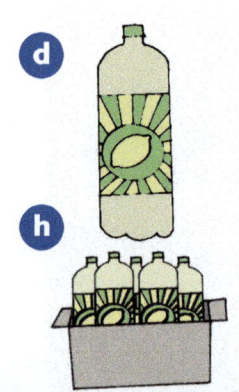

4 Listen and say the letter.

1 Can you take the dirty cups to the kitchen please, children? — b

a He wants her to make a cheese sandwich.

b She wants them to take the cups to the kitchen.

c He wants him to pass the bowl of salad.

d She wants him to hold the glass.

e They want her to open the bottle of lemonade.

f He wants them to put the glasses on the table.

5 Read and correct.

Paul wants to make lunch for his mom and dad. He wants his brother and sister to help him. He wants Vicky to make a bowl of salad, and then he wants her to make a bowl of soup. He wants Jack to take a plate of sandwiches and a bottle of lemonade to the table. After lunch he wants him to make a cup of coffee for their parents.
Paul wants to sit down and watch TV with a glass of apple juice. His brother and sister aren't happy, they're angry. They want Paul to help them.

1 Paul wants his mom and dad to help him.
2 He wants Vicky to make a box of noodles.
3 He wants her to make a cup of soup.
4 Paul wants Jack to take a plate of pancakes to the table.
5 He wants him to make a cup of coffee for their aunt and uncle.

6 Look, think, and answer.
1 What are the children doing?
2 Who's first?
3 Who's last?
4 Who's walking?

7 🎧 Listen and check.

8 🎧 Listen and say the name.

1 He's jumping the most quickly.

Alex.

LOOK

quickly	→	the **most quickly**
slowly	→	the **most slowly**
well	→	the **best**
badly	→	the **worst**

9 Look at the pictures. Find the differences.

> In picture B the clown's drinking a milkshake.

10 Complete the song. Listen and check.

> made   ate   wore   ~~said~~   drank   danced   gave   was

We had soup, We had pasta,
We had salad and cheese.
We all wanted more,
We all   said   "please."
We _____ presents,
And cards which we _____.
We _____ funny costumes,
We _____, and we played …

The party was good,
The party _____ great.
And now it's time to fly.
The party was good,
The party was great.

See you soon, goodbye.

The drinks we _____,
The food we _____.
The party was good,
The party was great.

We gave presents …

Now the party's over,
Now it's time to fly.
See you soon, goodbye.

11 Sing the song.

12 Sally's phonics

Say **soup** and **blue**,
And **think**, **thought**, and **flew**.
Say **wa**ter, **pas**ta, and **fea**ther,
And **par**ty, **bot**tle, and **wea**ther.
Another syllable will make it three,
Say **beau**tiful, **ele**phant and **care**fully!

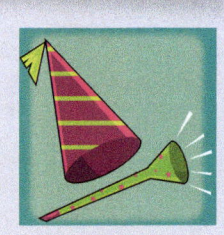

13 Choose a picture. Play the game.

What am I?

Do you have a red nose?

No, I don't.

Can you sail a boat?

Yes, I can.

14
CD3
LOCK & KEY
Let's go, Key! We have to work more carefully this time. We can't make any more mistakes.
ZOO
Eeek! No problem, Lock!
VROOOM!
Here, nice cat! Have a bag of parrot food! Mmmm!
Here's a bottle of water ...
No? How about a nice box of ... fruit?
ROAR! ROAR!
Look, there it is! The truck's over there!
City ZOO
Oh, yes. Now we got him!
We got you now, Nick. The police are coming to get you!
Oh, yes please. Take me away from the tiger. Thank you! You're my heroes.
Nice work, men. You caught Nick Motors for us!
City ZOO
Well, we had a little help.
No problem!

Science Food

Fact: A 60-gram bar of milk chocolate has seven teaspoons of sugar in it.

1 Look at the food plate.
How often do you think you need to eat food from each group?

- Fruit and vegetables
- Carbohydrates
- Protein
- Fats and sugars
- Dairy products

2 Read and answer.

For a healthy body we need to eat different kinds of food. There are five important groups of food: carbohydrates; dairy products; fats and sugars; protein; fruit and vegetables.

Carbohydrates give us energy. (1) What kinds of food are carbohydrates?

Dairy products make our bones and teeth strong because they contain calcium. We get calcium from milk and food that comes from milk, like yogurt. (2) Do you know another food that comes from milk?

Fats and sugars also give us energy, but a lot of fat and sugar is not good for our bodies. (3) What kinds of food have sugar? (4) What kinds of food have fat?

Protein is important because it is good for our muscles and makes them strong. Protein comes from animals and some vegetables, like beans. (5) What other foods do you think give us protein?

Fruit and vegetables have a lot of vitamins and minerals. (6) Can you say the names of five different fruits? (7) Can you name three different vegetables?

3 Read and match.

1 – e

Pasta salad

You need:
1. 2 tomatoes
2. 250 g pasta
3. 100 g cheese
4. 200 g chicken
5. 2 carrots
6. some lemon juice and oil

4 Read and order the sentences.

1 – f

Preparation:

a. Then cut the cheese into pieces and mix it in a big bowl with the tomatoes and carrots.

b. Now you can eat your pasta salad.

c. Next, cut the tomatoes and carrots into small pieces.

d. Second, cook the chicken. When it's cold, cut it into small pieces.

e. Last, put some oil and lemon juice over the salad.

f. First, cook the pasta in a lot of water.

g. Put the pasta and chicken into the bowl with the tomato, carrots, and cheese.

Project Write a recipe for your favorite lunch.

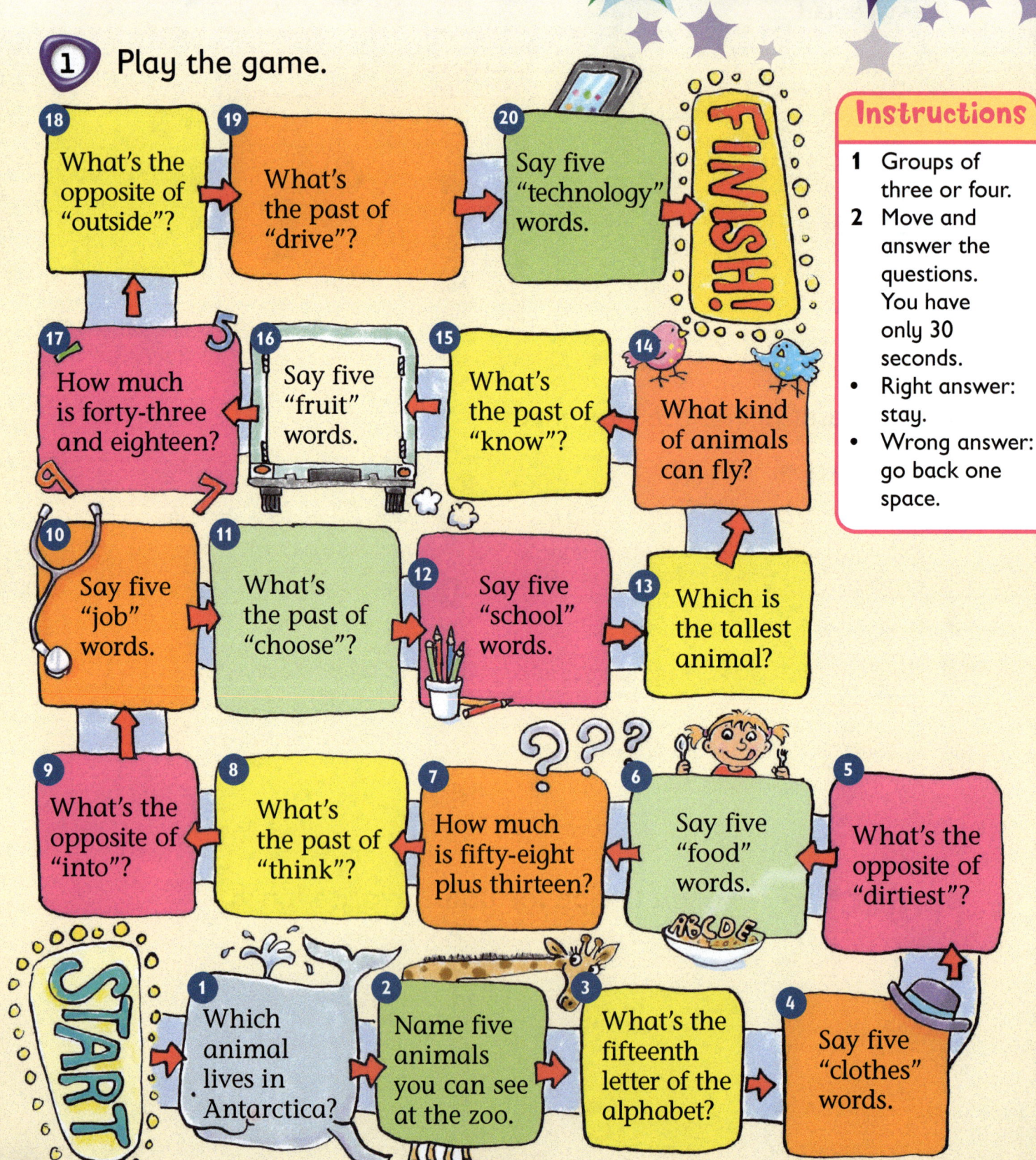

Review Units 7 and 8

1 Play the game.

Instructions

1. Groups of three or four.
2. Move and answer the questions. You have only 30 seconds.
- Right answer: stay.
- Wrong answer: go back one space.

START

1. Which animal lives in Antarctica?
2. Name five animals you can see at the zoo.
3. What's the fifteenth letter of the alphabet?
4. Say five "clothes" words.
5. What's the opposite of "dirtiest"?
6. Say five "food" words.
7. How much is fifty-eight plus thirteen?
8. What's the past of "think"?
9. What's the opposite of "into"?
10. Say five "job" words.
11. What's the past of "choose"?
12. Say five "school" words.
13. Which is the tallest animal?
14. What kind of animals can fly?
15. What's the past of "know"?
16. Say five "fruit" words.
17. How much is forty-three and eighteen?
18. What's the opposite of "outside"?
19. What's the past of "drive"?
20. Say five "technology" words.

FINISH!

80

2 Tell the story.

> Danny got up. He was sad. He wanted to play soccer outside, but the weather was terrible …

3 Now write the story.

Danny got up. He was sad. He wanted to play soccer outside, but the weather was terrible …

Quiz!

1 Who was in the Kid's Box Quiz Final?
2 What did the parrots do at the zoo?
3 What did Nick Motors take from the zoo?
4 What was there to eat at Scott's party?
5 Who jumped the most slowly in the sack race?
6 What did Nick Motors find inside the truck?

Units 1 & 2 — Values — Value others

1 Look and think. Say "yes" or "no."
1. When our friends help us in school, we say "sorry."
2. We can give flowers to people when we want to say thank you.
3. We say thank you to people when they help us.
4. When our parents give us a party, we say goodbye.

2 Listen and check.

3 Read and complete in pairs.

> our teacher.   them a letter.   and smile at them.
> ~~they help us.~~   say thank you.   give them a picture.

(We say thank you to people when …)   (they help us.)

1. We say thank you to people when …
2. We can give someone a present to …
3. When people help us, we can say thank you …
4. When we enjoy a school lesson, we can say thank you to …
5. When we want to say thank you to people, we can …
6. To say thank you to someone, we can sometimes write …

Be kind | **Values** | **Units 3 & 4**

1 Look and think. Say "yes" or "no."
1. We can give our seat to older people on the bus.
2. It's good to help younger children with a problem.
3. We can ask old people to carry our bags.
4. We can stay on the toys at the park when other children are waiting to use them.

2 🎧 Listen and check.

3 Read and match.
1. If we see old people on a bus or train, we can …
2. If we see small children with problems, we can …
3. If we see older people with a shopping bag, we can …
4. When other children want the same thing as us, …

a. carry it for them.
b. we can take turns.
c. try to help them.
d. stand up and give them our seat.

Units 5 & 6 Values — Be safe

1 Look and think. Say "yes" or "no."
1. You can play close to busy roads.
2. You can cross the road between cars.
3. You must stop, look, and listen before you cross the road.
4. You must wear a helmet when you ride a bike.

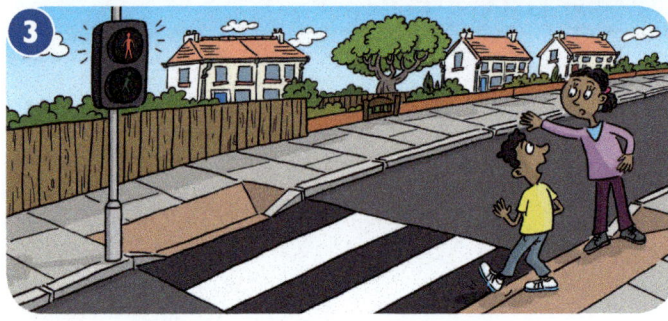

2 🔊 Listen and check.

3 Read and complete in pairs.

> use it to cross the road.   can't see you.   busy roads.
> ~~ride a bike.~~   before you cross the road.

"Remember to put on a helmet when you …"   "ride a bike."

1. Remember to put on a helmet when you …
2. Don't stand between cars when you cross the road. Drivers …
3. Don't play next to …
4. Remember to stop, look, and listen …
5. When there is a crosswalk, always …

Recycle **Values** **Units 7 & 8**

1 Look and think. Say "yes" or "no."
1. We must put plastic and paper into special bins.
2. We must not recycle glass.
3. We can make things from old clothes.
4. We must not recycle clothes.

2 🔊 Listen and check.

3 Read and match.
1. When we can't reuse things, we …
2. Make plastic bottles smaller …
3. Always put paper, glass, plastic, and cans …
4. We can make new things …

a. from old clothes.
b. into the right recycling bins.
c. before you recycle them.
d. can sometimes recycle them.

85

Grammar reference

Grandpa Star's older than Mr. Star.
The dog's bigger than the cat.
Uncle Fred's funnier than Aunt May.

He sometimes has to get up at five o'clock.
She always has to work on weekends.
He never has to do his homework on Saturday.

1
He's/She's the teacher who's wearing a red sweater.
They're the girls who are skipping rope.

2

What can I learn to do?	You can learn to sing.
What do you/they want to learn to do?	I/We/They want to learn to paint. I/We/They don't want to learn to roller-skate.
What does he/she want to learn to do?	He/She wants to learn to dance. He/She doesn't want to learn to ride a horse.
What's the Activity Center?	It's a place where you can learn to swim.

3

I/You/He/She/It/We/They	had / didn't have lunch at school.
Did you see the dentist last year? Did he/she eat chocolate cake?	Yes, I did. / No, I didn't. Yes, he/she did. / No, he/she didn't.
How many ice cream cones did you have?	I had two ice cream cones. / I didn't have an ice cream cone.

Her mom gave her medicine I had a drink They ate a sandwich	because	she had a headache. I was hot. they were hungry.

4

What did Alex need? Where did she live? Who did Mr. Burke stop? What did Scott carry?	Alex needed a hat and a scarf. She lived in a big town. Mr. Burke stopped Scott. Scott carried the boxes.

5

They were hungry,		they ate an apple.
It was cold,	so	they had a hot drink.
I couldn't find my map,		I got lost.

interesting → more interesting
famous → more famous
difficult → more difficult

This movie is more interesting than that one.
She is more famous than he is.
Math homework is more difficult than English homework.

My bike goes more slowly than yours.
He rides his bike more carefully than she does.

6

What did you buy?
Where did he put the DVD?
What did they think?
What did she know?

I bought / didn't buy a new MP3 player.
He put / didn't put it on the table.
They thought / didn't think the Internet was slow.
We knew / didn't know the song on the radio.

7

quick → quicker → the quickest
beautiful → more beautiful → the most beautiful
good → better → the best

It's the quickest lizard in the world.
Blue whales are the most beautiful animals.
I think rabbits are the best pets.

What did you eat?
What did he/she see?
Where did they/we swim?

I ate / didn't eat the cake.
He/She saw / didn't see a dolphin.
They/We swam / didn't swim in the ocean.

8

slowly → more slowly → the most slowly
carefully → more carefully → the most carefully

The woman's walking the most slowly.
The boys are riding the most carefully.

Movers practice test   Listening

Part 1   5 questions

Listen and draw lines. There is one example.

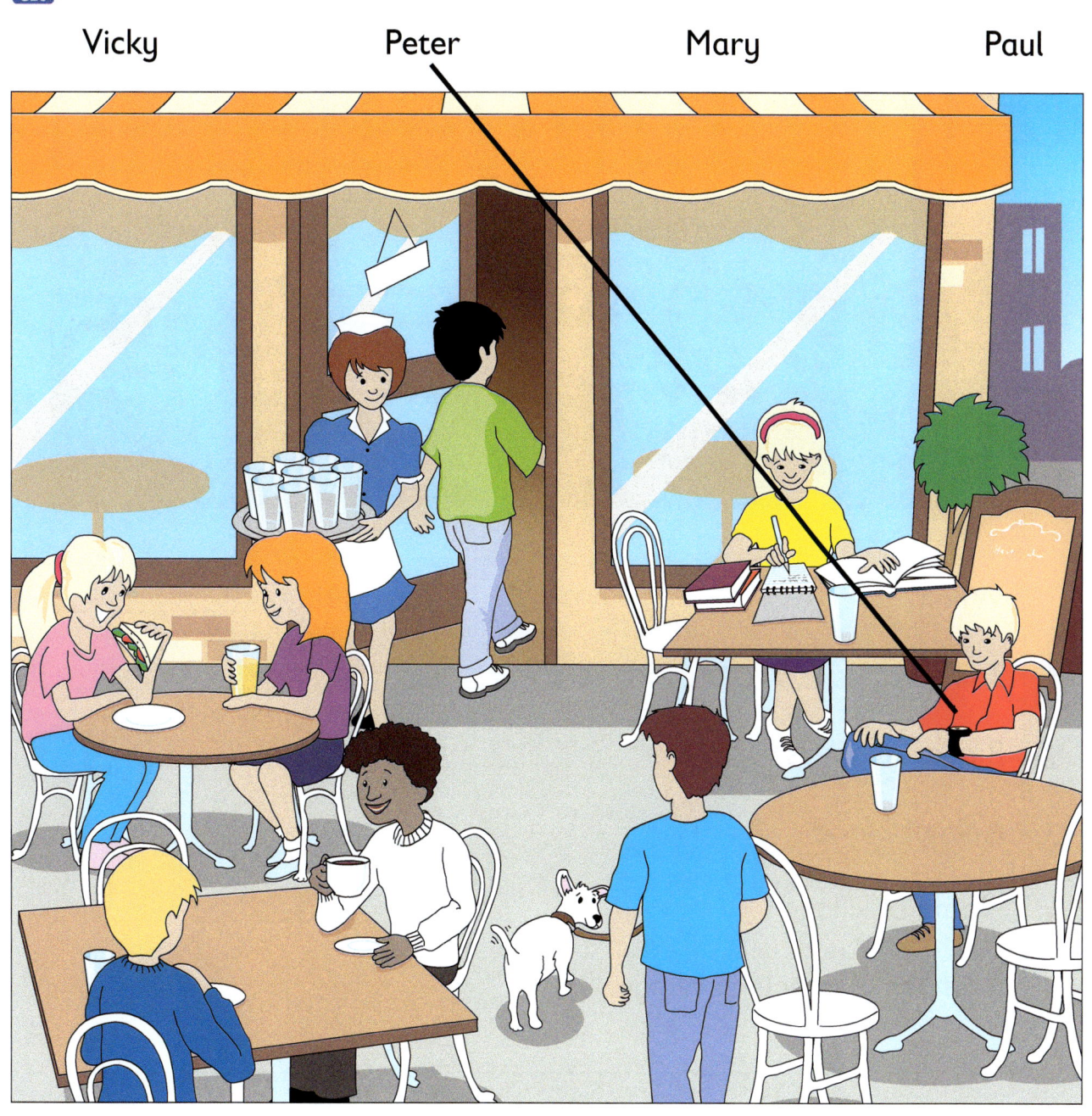

Vicky   Peter   Mary   Paul

Daisy   Jim   Fred

Part 2 5 questions

Listen and write. There is one example.

The village

	When?	_____Friday_____
1	Talked to	_____
2	Biggest animals	_____
3	Animals' food	_____
4	Name of village	_____
5	Number of people in village	_____

Part 3 5 questions

What sport does Peter do in these places?
Listen and write a letter in each box. There is one example.

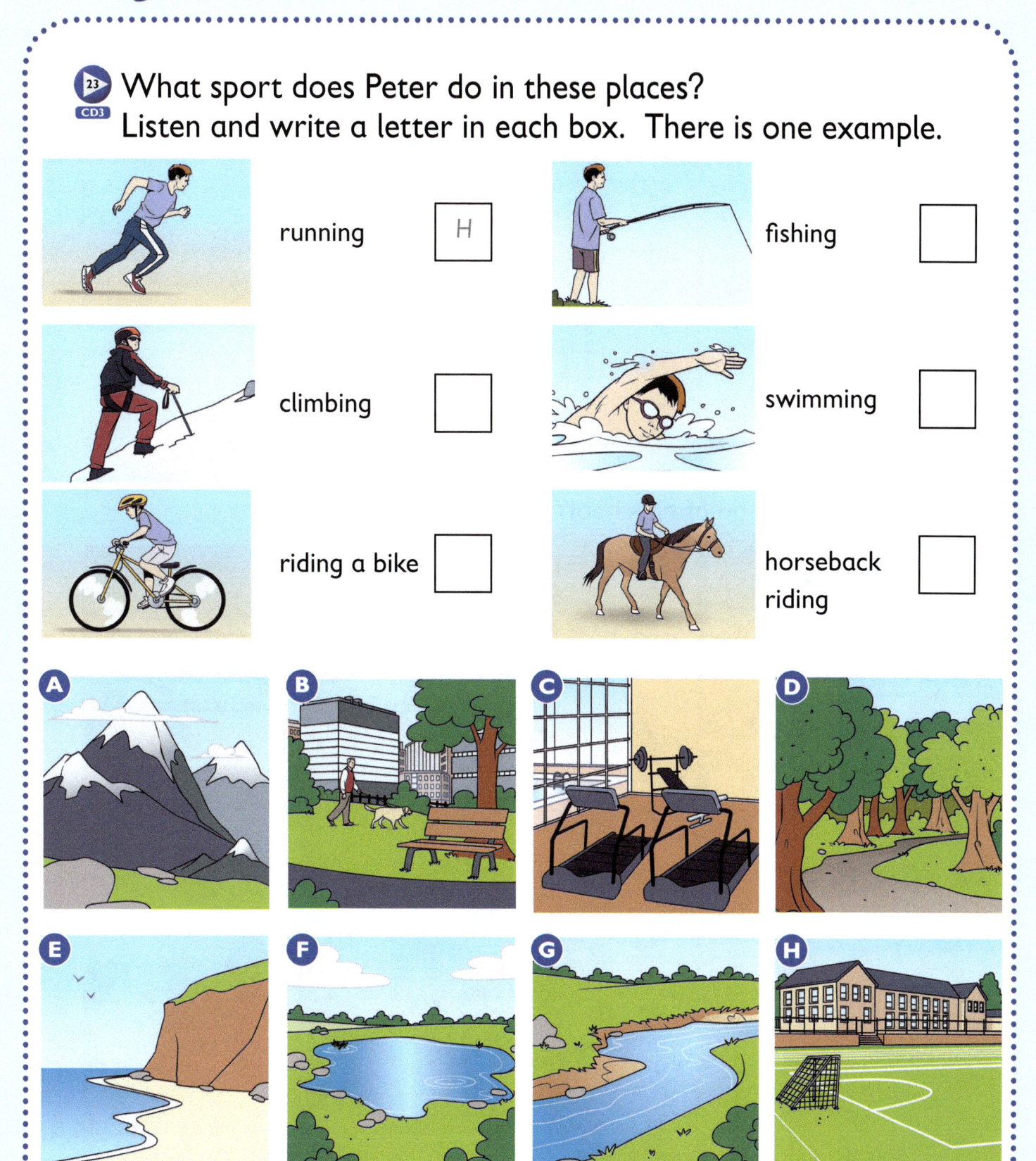

running — H

fishing — ☐

climbing — ☐

swimming — ☐

riding a bike — ☐

horseback riding — ☐

A B C D

E F G H

Part 4 5 questions

Listen and check (✓) the box. There is one example.

What was the weather like last weekend?

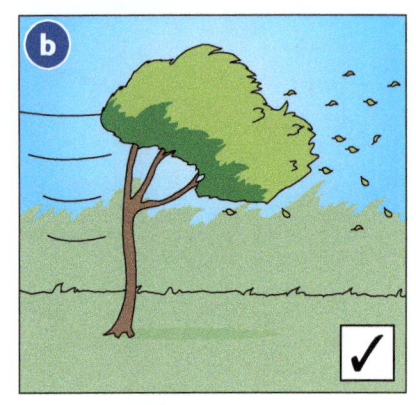

1 Where did Alex go after school?

2 What did they do at the party?

3 What did the man buy?

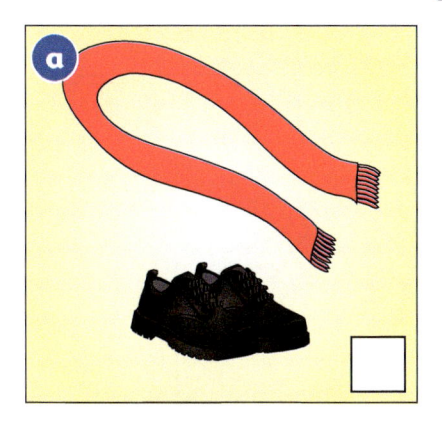

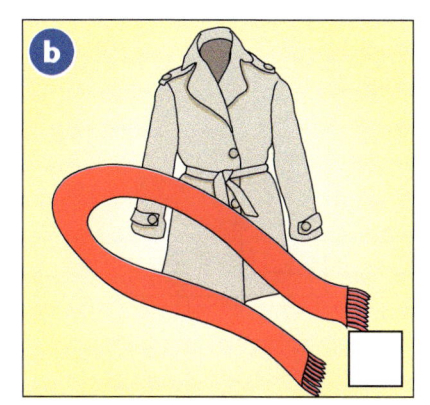

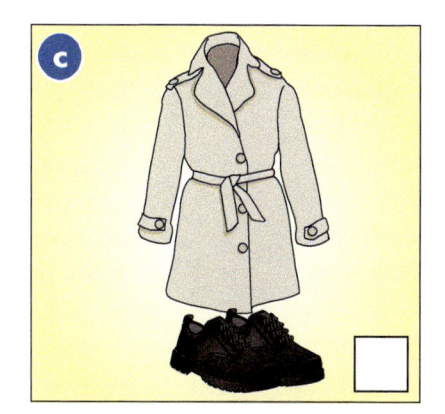

4 Where do the aliens live?

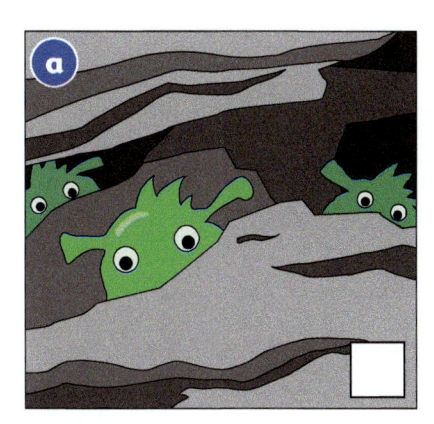

5 Which zoo animals did the girl like?

Part 5   5 questions

Listen and color and write. There is one example.

Movers practice test — Reading & Writing

Part 1 5 questions

Look and read. Choose the correct words and write them on the lines. There is one example.

a neck	 penguins	 kittens	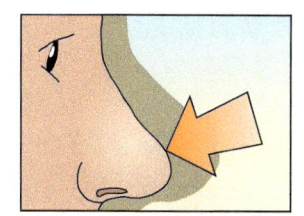 a nose
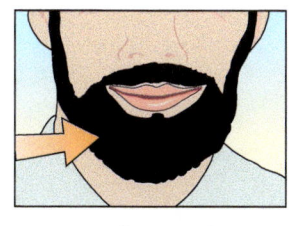 a beard	 rabbits	 mice	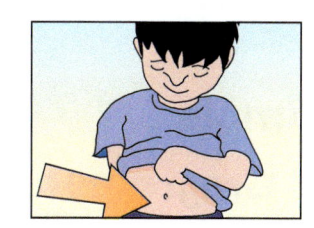 a stomach

Example

These pet animals are baby cats.   kittens

Questions

1 When you eat, your food and drink goes here.   _____
2 These animals can swim.   _____
3 This is between your head and your shoulders.   _____
4 This is on your face, between your eyes and
   your mouth.   _____
5 These animals have big ears. They eat grass.   _____

Part 2 6 questions

Read the text and choose the best answer.

Example

Miss Gray: Hello, Jack. Why are you sitting there?
Jack:
- **A** I can't walk home.
- **B** It doesn't work.
- **C** I'm not walking.

Questions

1 Miss Gray: Oh dear! What's the matter?
Jack:
- **A** It doesn't matter.
- **B** I hurt my foot.
- **C** It hurt me.

2 Miss Gray: When did you do that?
Jack:
- **A** After school this afternoon.
- **B** I didn't do it.
- **C** I'm sorry.

3 Miss Gray: Don't cry! I can help you. Where do you live?
Jack: A It's a big house.
   B At home.
   C On Bath Street.

4 Miss Gray: Is there a bus to your house?
Jack: A No, I don't have a ticket.
   B No, we always walk.
   C No, but I like going by bus.

5 Miss Gray: Do you have your cell phone with you?
Jack: A No. He doesn't have one.
   B No. I lost it yesterday.
   C No. There isn't a cell phone.

6 Miss Gray: Well, do you want to call your mom?
Jack: A Yes, please!
   B Yes, you do.
   C Yes, it would.

Part 3 6 questions

Read the story. Choose a word from the box.
Write the correct word next to numbers 1–5.
There is one example.

The *Flying Shark* was a very famous pirate ship. Everyone was afraid of the pirates from this ship. But one day they got lost. They ……… *sailed* ……… to an island to look for treasure. They looked and looked, but they couldn't find any because there was a mistake on their **(1)** ……………………… . They were on the wrong island! The pirates were very **(2)** ……………………… .
In the morning it was very hot but there was nothing to eat or drink. Now they didn't want treasure. They wanted food and **(3)** ……………………… .
Then they heard someone calling to them from the trees. It said, "Coconuts and bananas. Coconuts and bananas." The pirates ran to see who it was. But it wasn't a person, it was some **(4)** ……………………… . There were lots of coconuts and bananas in the trees. They **(5)** ……………………… the bananas and drank milk from the coconuts.
"This is better than treasure," they said.

Example

sailed	beach	water
map	read	angry
happy	parrots	ate

(6) Now choose the best name for the story.
Check one box.

The beautiful treasure ☐

The terrible weather ☐

The hungry pirates ☐

Part 4 5 questions

Read the text. Choose the correct words and write them on the lines.

Sharks

Example	Sharks are fish. They ……… don't ……… like cold water.
1	They live in the ocean in hot parts ………………… the world. They catch smaller fish and sea animals, that they
2	………………… with their strong teeth. Some people say that sharks never fall asleep, but this is
3	wrong. They sleep, but ………………… eyes are always
4	open and they never stop ………………… . There are many different kinds of sharks. The biggest
5	ones are white. People ………………… afraid of them, but most sharks are small, and they can't hurt you.

Example	doesn't	don't	didn't
1	on	at	of
2	ate	eat	eaten
3	her	its	their
4	moving	moves	move
5	is	are	be

Part 5 7 questions

Look at the pictures and read the story.
Write some words to complete the sentences about the story. You can use 1, 2, or 3 words.

A nice Saturday

"What can I do?" Jane asked her mom on Saturday morning. "Let's go to the supermarket!" Mom said. "We can go shopping and then make lunch." "I hate shopping," Jane said. "It's boring."

"OK," Mom said, "I have a better idea." She called Jane's grandma. "Bring Jane to me," Grandma said. "I love having her here."

They got in the car and drove to Grandma's apartment. Grandma opened the door and said, "Come on, Jane, we should go shopping. Let's buy some nice food."

Examples

Mom wanted to go to the supermarket on ___Saturday morning___.

Jane didn't want to go ___shopping___ with her mom.

Questions

1 Mom had a good _____, and she called Jane's grandma.

2 Mom took Jane to Grandma's apartment by _____.

Grandma took Jane to a market on the street near her apartment. They bought lots of good things – vegetables, pasta, bread, and a bottle of juice.
Jane carried it all in a big bag. She took it upstairs carefully.

3 Jane and Grandma bought lots of nice things to eat at _____.

4 They put all the food in _____ and carried it to Grandma's apartment.

Grandma cooked the pasta. Jane made a salad. "It's sunny today," Grandma said. "Let's eat on the balcony." They sat and enjoyed their lunch. "I like your salad, Jane," Grandma said. "It's very good." Then Mom called. "I'm having a great day," Jane told her. "We went shopping and made lunch." Mom laughed. "'Oh, Jane, you are funny!" she said.

5 Jane and Grandma had lunch on _____.

6 The _____ that Jane made was very good.

7 Mom thought it was _____ when Jane said, "I'm having a great day."

Part 6 6 questions

Look and read and write.

Examples

The woman has <u>curly black</u> hair.
What is the small girl playing with? <u>two toy cars</u>

Complete the sentences

1 The man _____ soccer with a boy.
2 The woman and the girl are sitting _____ .

Answer the questions

3 Where is the cat? _____
4 What are the girl and boy with blond hair wearing on their feet?
_____

Now write two sentences about the picture.

5 _____
6 _____